A TOUR OF THE CAUSEWAY COAST

For my sons and daughters

This book has received financial support from the Cultural Traditions Programme of the Community Relations Council which aims to encourage acceptance and understanding of cultural diversity.

The Friar's Bush Press
24 College Park Avenue
Belfast BT7 1LR
Published 1990

ISBN 0 946872 39 2

Printed by W. & G. Baird Ltd., Antrim

The photographs
Front Cover: Causeway Tram at Dunluce (WAG 1875)
Back Cover: On the strand, Portrush (WAG 502)

The WAG numbers after each photograph refer to the collection at the Ulster Folk and Transport Museum from whom prints may be obtained.

A TOUR OF THE
Causeway Coast

*Historic photographs from
the W. A. Green Collection
in the Ulster Folk and
Transport Museum.*

Cahal Dallat

LADIES' SWIMMING POOL, PORTRUSH.   W.A.G.505.

Introduction

The photographer, William Alfred Green, is probably best known for having recorded many of the farming practices and rural customs of Ulster but he also had an eye for buildings—whether single cottages on the landscape or groups of buildings in villages and towns. He came to the north coast in the first three decades of the twentieth century. This was a time when the seaside resorts of Ballycastle, Portrush and Portstewart were blossoming and the recently opened electric tram, operating between Portrush to the Giant's Causeway, was still a subject of wonderment.

Our tour begins with scenic views of historic Ballycastle which was designated a "conservation area" in 1990. It seems strange that Green did not include in his north coast selection a view of the ruins of Dunaneanie Castle (the first home of the MacDonnells of Antrim) perched on the cliff-top to the west of the town. Perhaps he travelled by the inland road to Ballintoy, as he managed to ignore Clare Park House, the home of the McGildowneys, and Kenbane Castle, built about 1544 by Colla MacDonnell, whose marriage to Evelyn MacQuillan of Dunluce Castle was to lead to the Battle of Orra in 1559.

It is evident from the number of photographs which he took that Carrick-a-Rede Rope Bridge held a certain fascination for him as it does for so many people.

Ballintoy with its sea stacks and thatched cottages was a particularly good subject for his skill, but one wonders why he did not turn his tripod towards the harbour proper and its limestone pier from which basalt square setts and limestone were being exported when he was on his rounds.

Whitepark Bay with its golden strand was an obvious target for his lens as was the miniature village of Portbraddan with its miniscule church.

It would be difficult to ignore Dunseverick Castle perched as it is on a basaltic outcrop, but few people are aware of picturesque Dunseverick harbour which Green has managed to preserve on film.

He was also attracted by the Giant's Causeway and managed to capture the outstanding features such as the Honeycomb, the Organ, the Fan, the Wishing Chair and the Loom. Many of the views appear at first sight to be duplicates but it may be that they were taken on different occasions. With the many changes which have taken place at the Causeway it is important to have such a collection of photographs as Green's to record how it used to be.

No photographic record of the Causeway would be complete without a picture of the hotels and the electric tramway. Kane's Royal Hotel has since been demolished making Green's picture an even more valuable record.

No visitor to the north coast can afford to ignore Dunluce Castle, which, while not being the oldest castle in Ulster, is probably the most impressive and the one with the most tales of romance, jealousy, bravery and treachery.

Green's photography has managed to encapsulate the "day-tripperish" bustle and excitement of Portrush which had been described as early as 1837 as "a favourite place of resort for strangers, particularly during the bathing season". It would have been interesting, however, to have had another picture of the Northern Counties Hotel to which the staff and pupils of Campbell College were evacuated during World War II, and Fawcett's Royal Hotel which welcomed the staff and students of Stranmillis Training College in the same period.

Green's black and white photographs ideally portray the peaceful and relaxing character of Portstewart which John Cromie had been so anxious to preserve. Much of this pleasant resort would qualify for designation as a conservation area.

I trust that Green's photographs and the accompanying commentary will enable the reader to travel back along memory lane.

Cahal Dallat

HARBOUR ROAD, BALLYCASTLE (WAG 2494)

The proper name for this road is Quay Road but irrespective of what it is called, it is certainly one of the most beautiful roads in Ireland. With trees and gardens along each side, framing the vista of the blue waters of the Sea of Moyle, the view is breath-taking. Hugh Boyd, the landlord of Ballycastle, who laid out the streets of the town in the 1740s certainly appreciated the scenic beauty of the area. Boyd's planning was recognised in June 1990 when Ballycastle (including Quay Road) was designated a conservation area by the Department of the Environment.

2

CASTLE HILL AND STRAND, BALLYCASTLE (WAG 829)

What our photographer, W. A. Green, calls Castle Hill is better known as Quay Hill but he was probably aware that the ruins of Dunaneanie Castle stood on the headland at the top of the hill. On the left of the picture is Ballycastle's largest hotel, the Marine. Built in 1889, it was destroyed by terrorist bombs in 1979. In the centre the coastguard station with its imposing tower gives the impression that it was some form of fortification. The last house at the top of the hill is White Lodge from which Marconi's first wireless messages across the sea to Rathlin Island were to be the fore-runner of world-wide broadcasting as we know it today.

BALLYCASTLE FROM GLENSHESK (WAG 2062A)

Ballycastle is made up of three villages—the Quay (or seaside resort), the Diamond (or market precinct) and the Milltown (or industrial area). This is a photograph of the Quay and the fields in the foreground were incorporated in the 1920s into the Ballycastle Golf Course which had been opened in 1890. The mound of Dunamallaght (the fort of the curse) stands among the trees on the left. In 1857 when the Margey Bridge in the centre of the photograph was being built, the builders had great difficulty in establishing a proper foundation because of 'running sand'. They solved the problem by laying down large sacks of sheeps' wool and building on them. One hundred and thirty three years later the bridge is still standing.

KNOCKLAYD MOUNTAIN, BALLYCASTLE (WAG 830)

Knocklayd Mountain (1695 feet) is the second highest in County Antrim and the name means "the broad mountain". In spite of its lack of height it provides excellent shelter for the beautiful town of Ballycastle which lies at its foot. A bog-burst on the mountain in May 1788 was reported in the Dublin papers as a volcanic eruption in which *the lava flowed for 39 hours and twenty-seven persons perished.* Details of this incident continued to be reported in the papers for several days and it was some time before it was discovered to be an elaborate hoax.

ROPE BRIDGE, CARRICK-A-REDE (WAG 1629)

The name Carrick-a-Rede means "the rock in the passageway" and refers to the path taken by the salmon on their return to the rivers in which they have been spawned. As a result, the salmon which have been hugging the coast have to swim round the rock and in the process they swim into the salmon nets. The rope-bridge is erected every spring to enable the fishermen to cross to their daily work at the salmon fishery.

This picture with the three fishermen standing on the bridge on their way back from the fishery, gives some idea of the depth of the chasm. The bridge is shown with only a single rope handrail. Yet fishermen think nothing of crossing daily, often with a heavy basket of fish on their backs although one false step on the planking could mean a fall of ninety feet into the sea below. As the bridge swings and sways with each step, crossing it is not for the faint-hearted or light-headed.

SWINGING BRIDGE, CARRICK-A-REDE (WAG 838)

Perhaps it was because of the fact that tourists wanted to cross the bridge that a second rope handrail was added. Nevertheless this lady in her Edwardian costume is to be admired for having crossed the bridge in the early part of the century. Crossing the bridge is commonplace today—perhaps we live in a more adventurous age. At least one man has crossed it on a bicycle and Charlie Hamill, a Ballycastle man, was photographed doing handstands in the middle of the bridge some twenty years ago.

BALLINTOY VILLAGE, CO. ANTRIM (WAG 181)

Ballintoy was originally a linear clachan with the single street or road dividing the upland pasture or common grazing on the inland side from the strip fields running towards the sea on the other. The Carrick-a-Rede Hotel, one of the main buildings in the village, had been built by Edmund (better known as Ned) McCambridge, the proprietor of the Boyd Arms Hotel in Ballycastle. When he became the owner of the Antrim Arms Hotel in Ballycastle, P. J. O'Carrigan took over the Carrick-a-Rede Hotel. McCambridge continued to run excursions to Ballintoy and the Giant's Causeway and it is likely that the two long cars or wagonettes parked outside the hotel had brought tourists from the Antrim Arms Hotel.

BALLINTOY, CO. ANTRIM (WAG 2861)

A similar view, but this time the focus is on Ballintoy's other hotel—the Fullerton Arms. It was the custom to name the local hotel after the landlord. Several hotels on the Antrim coast were named after the Earl of Antrim. The Stewarts of Ballintoy Castle were the local landlords but by the mid-eighteenth century the estate was mortgaged and subsequently purchased by Dr Alexander Fullerton of Jamaica whose forebears came from north Antrim. A Model T Ford stands besides Ballintoy's first petrol pump and the building beyond was the police barracks. The end of the street climbs steeply up Knocksoghey.

BALLINTOY HARBOUR AND SEA-STACKS (WAG 2937)

This area is referred to as Ballintoy Harbour although the harbour proper is at the photographer's back. The largest outcrop of rock in the background is Dunshammer (the fort of the shamrocks)—an Iron Age fort which had an artificially flattened top. The smaller rocks which are sea-stacks or basaltic extrusions have descriptive names like Islandforglass (which means the cold grey island) and Islandoo (black island).

BALLINTOY HARBOUR (WAG 2938)

The attractive thatched cottages nestle snugly into the shelter of the rugged limestone and basalt cliffs. This was once the home of a well-known fishing family—the Rourkes (local pronunciation Rooricks). Their sturdy, clinker-built boats lay conveniently within sight of the cottages. The O'Rourkes were chieftains in the Galway region and it is believed that the Ballintoy Rourkes had come north with Colla MacDonnell's mercenaries in the sixteenth century.

CLIFFS OF LARRIBAN, BALLINTOY (WAG 3675)

The beauty of the Antrim coast depends on the interplay of black and white provided by the juxtaposition of the limestone and basalt cliffs. The white headland here is Larryban and the name in Gaelic *Laitreach ban* means the white fort, referring to the existence of an Iron Age fort. This headland no longer exists having been quarried away in the 1950s with permission from the Northern Ireland Ministry of Commerce to provide lime products for agriculture and building. It could not happen today—or could it?

MOUNT DRUID CROMLEACH, BALLINTOY (WAG 178)

Cromleachs are dotted all over the Irish landscape. The name Mount Druid suggests that people once believed that dolmens and cromleachs were places where druids worshipped. Ironically the Church of Ireland rectory close by used to be known as Mount Druid because of its proximity to the stone. Other cromleachs in the area include Clegnagh (which means the place of skulls) and Cloughnabohill (the rock of the boy). Extensive bauxite mines were worked in the nearby townland of Lemnagh about one hundred years ago.

WHITEPARK BAY (WAG 182)

One of the most beautiful strands on the north coast stretches from Ballintoy to Portbraddan — Whitepark Bay strand. The area can also claim to be one of the most important Stone Age settlements in Ulster, where Stone Age man discovered a plentiful source of supply of flints for the manufacture of flintscrapers, knives and other essential tools. Pieces of unfinished scrapers can still be found in the sand dunes at the back of the beach. A stream or burn running down the strand exposes lias formations which contain the remains of many fossils.

PORTBRADDAN FROM WHITEPARK BAY (WAG 846)

The small village of Portbraddan nestles in a sheltered cove at the west end of Whitepark Bay. Approached by a steep winding road, it reminds one of Cornish villages such as the Looe or Polperro. The name of Portbraddan means the "port of the salmon" and a successful salmon fishery is still being operated here. Ireland's smallest church — St Goban's Church of Ireland—is tucked in under the cliffs.

PORTBRADDAN AND THE WHITE CLIFFS OF WHITEPARK BAY (WAG 3310)

On the headland above the village lie the ruins of the old church of Templastragh. The name means the "church of the light" and according to a local legend, when the church was being built, each day's stonework was thrown down at night. Subsequently a light began to appear at night and when the builders were persuaded to move their operation to the area of the light, there was no further problem with the stonework.

WHITEPARK BAY (WAG 2221)

This view from the west shows traces of several duns or forts and the area where Stone Age man had his "flint factory". The building in the foreground, which subsequently became the Whitepark Bay youth hostel, was formerly a school. To all appearances it was very little better than a hedge school and yet it provided the early education for such important personages as Edward McNaghten, Lord of the Treasury, Sir Francis McNaghten, chief justice of Calcutta and the Honourable Robert Stewart, afterwards to become the famous Lord Castlereagh.

DUNSEVERICK VILLAGE (WAG 1800)

Dunseverick village is the perfect example of a clachan with the yard or street running along between the houses. At the end of the street can be seen a house, built at right angles to the others, to provide some shelter from the prevailing winds. The houses are roofed with roped thatch, a Scotch cart stands on the left, while a jaunting car completes the picture on the right.

BENGORE HEAD FROM DUNSEVERICK HARBOUR
(WAG 2901A)

The basaltic headlands of north Antrim all have similar profiles—a perpendicular cliff in the top half and a forty-five degree, sloping block scree in the lower half. Bengore Head, which means the "headland of the goats", is a perfect example of this profile. The calm water of Dunseverick Harbour provides a safe haven for the two boats whose registrations are CE 58 and CE 55—CE being the first and last letters of the port of registration, Coleraine.

DUNSEVERICK HARBOUR (WAG 2883)

The same families have always fished out of Dunseverick Harbour—the Gaults, the McMullans, the McClellands, the Wilkinsons, the McKays. The men working at lines and nets are (from the right) William John Gault, James Gault, Bob Gault and William McClelland. The boats, which are Norwegian style clinker-built dronheims, were at one time very popular with fishermen on the Antrim coast. They were probably built in Kellys boatyard in Portrush.

DUNSEVERICK CASTLE (WAG 848)

Dunseverick Castle, the oldest castle in Ulster, derived its name from the Gaelic *Dun Soibhairce* meaning Severick's fort. Severick controlled the portion of Ireland north of a line drawn from Drogheda to Galway. At a later period the castle was the terminus of the great north road, the Sliabh Miodluachra, which ran from Tara, the residence of the High King, to Dunseverick. The O'Cahans occupied the castle from about 1237 until 1657.

THE GIANT'S CAUSEWAY FROM THE SEA (WAG 155)

The Giant's Causeway has so many separate features that it is impossible to photograph them all at one time. W. A. Green has captured a picture which gives a very good general impression of the columnar Causeway and the surrounding cliffs. There are said to be forty thousand perpendicular columns of various heights in the Causeway area. In an attempt to restore the Causeway to its natural appearance, the house and railings in the picture have been removed by the National Trust which controls the Causeway.

THE HONEYCOMB, GIANT'S CAUSEWAY (WAG 153)

The most easily recognised section of the Giant's Causeway is the honeycomb. This is probably because it is featured in so many advertisements for tourism, motor-cars, liquid refreshment and various other products. It is here that the columns with their four, five, six, seven, eight and even nine sides can be seen at their best.

THE ORGAN, GIANT'S CAUSEWAY (WAG 3874)

This formation is clearly reminiscent of the pipes of a grand organ. According to local legend, Finn MacCool, the giant who built the Causeway, is said to have made this organ for his son, Ossian, the warrior poet, to play upon and to accompany his songs. It was believed that when the wind was in the right direction, his music could be heard by the Grey Man, the storm-god of Fairhead, near Ballycastle.

THE AMPHITHEATRE AND CHIMNEY TOPS, GIANT'S CAUSEWAY (WAG 842)

To the east of the Causeway lies a beautiful semi-circular bay called the Giant's Amphitheatre. Its background is made up of several tiers of gigantic pillars towering above each other, the crowning tier being composed of a row of columns eighty feet high. Further to the east stand the Chimney Tops, the tallest of which is forty feet high.

Oral tradition had it that the captain of the Armada ship, the *Girona*, had mistaken the Chimney Tops for Dunluce Castle and ordered his men to fire at them; and that the rebound from the cannons had driven the ship on to a rock.

PORT NA SPANIA, GIANT'S CAUSEWAY (WAG 158)

It was an erroneous theory that the Spanish galleas, *Girona*, had fired at the Chimney Tops mistaking them for Dunluce Castle. The 28th October 1558 was a very stormy night, and the *Girona*, with a damaged rudder and over one thousand men on board, was being driven along by a strong north-west wind. It is possible that the captain, Don Alonso de Leveyia, was trying to keep as close as possible to the shore seeking shelter, when the ship ran on to Lacada Point—a partially-submerged rock stretching out into the sea. There were only eleven survivors. The place where the bodies were washed ashore is still known as Port na Spaniagh (the port of the Spaniards).

GIANT'S CAUSEWAY (WAG 3876)

There is a tradition that the Giant's Causeway was built by the Irish giant, Finn MacCoul, who wished to make a causeway across to Scotland, where he intended to fight the Scottish giant. About the end of the seventeenth century the Royal Society in London began to take a scientific interest in what was being described as *"the eighth wonder of the world".* Among the learned papers of the Society was one on the Causeway presented by Sir Richard Bulkley. Dr Lyster was also concerned in 1693 and Dr Thomas Mollineaux, who died in 1733, carried out considerable research on the subject. It is possible to learn the full story of the Causeway and its volcanic origins in the prize-winning interpretative centre established there by Moyle District Council.

WISHING CHAIR, GIANT'S CAUSEWAY (WAG 362)

The Giant's Causeway has always been an attractive subject for artists. As early as 1740 Susanna Drury exhibited two paintings of the Causeway in Dublin and engravings of these paintings were made in 1743. In spite of this artistic interest Dr Samuel Johnston, the celebrated English writer said of the Causeway that "It was worth seeing but not worth going to see." Dr Johnston's comment was contradicted by the fact that the Causeway was declared a World Heritage site by UNESCO in 1987. The visitor to the Causeway is struck by the regularity of the stonework. There is something so artificial about the whole scene, that it is at first very hard to realise that it is natural, and not man-made. It seems the most natural thing in the world then to sit in the wishing chair and make a wish. At one time it was necessary to purchase a glass of water from the old lady in charge of the Giant's Well at the price of one penny, if one's wish was to be granted.

LORD ANTRIM'S PARLOUR, GIANT'S CAUSEWAY
(WAG 160)

The Giant's Causeway became a tourist attraction in the days when only the wealthy could afford to be tourists. Lord Antrim's Parlour, this circular group of pillars, is supposed to have received its name when Lord Antrim entertained a party of friends there. Other features named were the Lady's Fan because of its shape, the Giant's Eyeglass, the Hawk's Head, the Priest and his Flock, the King and his Nobles, the Lover's Leap, the Four Sisters (four pillars), the Giant's Peephole and the Giant's Granny (a single column).

THE CHIMNEY TOPS, GIANT'S CAUSEWAY (WAG 161)

There is a pathetic story told about the Chimney Tops. It was said that a boy of weak intellect in the district lost his mother to whom he was greatly attached, and that he used to spend his days at her grave. A friend told him that his mother had gone up to Heaven, so he asked "How high is Heaven? Is it as high as the Organ?" "Oh aye" came the reply "higher than the Chimney Tops!" The following evening the boy was seen climbing towards the summit of the Chimney Tops, and the alarm was raised. There was nothing, however, that anyone could do and when darkness fell the people went home expecting to find the boy lying dead in the morning. Unbelievably he managed to climb down at first light and returned to his home.

THE HARBOUR, GIANT'S CAUSEWAY (WAG 845)

It would be unusual today to see nets drying at the Causeway or fourteen boats drawn up waiting to be hired by tourists. Times have changed and tourists no longer have the time to visit Port Cuan in a rowing boat or be regaled by the stories of the boatman. That treat belongs to a more leisurely age. Anyone wishing to re-live the history of Port na Spaniagh and Lacada Point need no longer travel there by rowing boat but may do so in relative comfort by walking along the National Trust's cliff path.

PORT NOFFER, GIANT'S CAUSEWAY (WAG 363)

Port Noffer (the giant's port or bay) is the Gaelic name for the Causeway. The small bays along the Causeway all have Gaelic names e.g. Portnaboe (the cow's port), Port Ganny (sandy port), Port Reostan (port of the king's dining room), Portnacallian (the girls' port), Port na Tober (port of the spring well) where German submarines were said to have obtained fresh water in World War I, Port na Gaethe (the windy port), Port na Truin (port of sorrow, because of the sound made by the sea passing in and out of a subterranean cave below the cliffs), Pleaskinn (the dry headland) and lots more.

PORT COON, GIANT'S CAUSEWAY (WAG 3414)

Port Cuan (the port of the harbour) like most other caves has a certain air of mystery about it. It was to be expected that tourists would be keen to visit it and no doubt they were encouraged by the many stories and legends which the boatmen told them. The cave is forty feet high and boats can penetrate it for one hundred and fifty yards. The interior resembles a gothic cathedral and at one time it was the custom for a pistol to be fired or a bugle to be blown so that the visitors could be thrilled by the powerful echo.

PORTRUSH/GIANT'S CAUSEWAY TRAM (WAG 2935)

The Giant's Causeway Tram, which has always been referred to as the first hydro-electric tramway in the world, completed its ten mile journey from Portrush, at the terminus near the Causeway Hotel. This hotel was owned by Mr William A. Traill, who had been the engineer of the Causeway Tramway, and only porters from his hotel were allowed into the tramway terminal. Passengers for Kane's Hotel had to carry their own luggage to the road before being met by the hotel porters. As might be expected there was always friction between the hotels.

THE CAUSEWAY HOTELS (WAG 3425)

The Causeway Hotel (on the left) had an advantage over Kane's Hotel (on the right) in that it was lighted by electricity from the power station at Bushmills which supplied the power for the Causeway Tram. When the Prince of Wales (later Edward VII) visited the Causeway, Mrs Frank Kane of Kane's Hotel took him in for tea and asked for permission to call her hotel "The Royal Hotel."

Prices of meals in 1887

Breakfast and Luncheon . . . . .1/-, 1/6 and 2/-
Dinner . . . . .1/6, 2/- and 2/6
Single bedroom 2/-
Double bedroom 3/6

SALMON LEAP, BUSHMILLS (WAG 963)

This picture clearly illustrates how the River Bush was named. The name derives from the Gaelic *buaise* meaning "torrential" and there are certainly many cataracts and waterfalls on the River Bush as it makes its journey from Altnahinch Dam to the sea near Portballintrae. It is one of Ulster's finest salmon rivers.

SALMON LEAP ON THE RIVER BUSH (WAG 962)

Just another illustration of the "torrential river" at one of the finest fishing stretches of the Bush. The river had a commercial importance, however, as it provided water-power for a number of mills in the village — hence the name Bushmills. The mills included a flax-mill, a corn-mill, a paper-mill and a spade-mill, which is seen here. The flax-mill later became the generating station which supplied the electricity for the Giant's Causeway Tram.

MAIN STREET, BUSHMILLS (WAG 960)

Bushmills village was a settlement dependent on its mills and it did not begin to grow until 1828 when Sir Francis McNaghten built the market place and grain stores seen here on the left beyond the clock tower. Markets were held each week on Tuesdays and Fridays. The tall building on the right is the courthouse, also built by Sir Francis, and no doubt the square, in the centre of which the 1914-1918 War Memorial stands, was part of his planning.

MAIN STREET, BUSHMILLS (WAG 3423)

The market tower is a prominent feature of the main street whether one looks east or west. Just out of the picture on the extreme left is the courthouse. Old and new forms of transport stand near each other — a jaunting car and a motor-car (possibly a Morris Cowley). The large house on the left on the far side of the square was the focus for an alternative form of transport — "The Dunluce Cycle Works". Bushmills also had "The Bush Cycle Works" higher up Main Street. The small houses at the far end of the street were known as "Nailmakers Row" in the days when nail-making was a cottage industry.

THE BRIDGE AND HOTEL, BUSHMILLS (WAG 961)

The bridge in any town is a recognised meeting place for a yarn. The two elderly gentlemen at the right hand end of the bridge, seem to be more interested in spotting a fresh-run Bush salmon. The hotel with its sturdy basaltic stonework, claimed in its advertisements that it was *"convenient for anglers on the River Bush".* The steps leading from the hotel down to the river would seem to verify this claim.

SOUTERRAIN, BUSHMILLS' WEE FOLKS CAVE (WAG 818)

The belief in fairies was strong in north Antrim even among the Scottish settlers and inevitably souterrains and other underground tunnels were seen as "wee folks caves". It was always considered wise to refer to fairies as the wee folk, the gentle folk or the gentle people, as it was known that they were easily offended and to offend them was to invite trouble.

PORTBALLINTRAE (WAG 2932)

Portballintrae can claim to be one of the most delightful seaside resorts on the north coast. The houses which formed the original village were built in a line along the shore and all of them had a fine view of the sea. When it became known in the middle of the nineteenth century that salt-water had medicinal qualities, sea-bathing became very popular and the landed gentry built bathing lodges. Seaport Lodge was built at Portballintrae by the Leslies of Leslie Hill, Ballymoney. The broad strand gave Portballintrae its name, which means "the port of the town of the strand."

PORTBALLINTRAE (WAG 2217A)

In this picture the sand has begun to recede and today the sand has almost totally disappeared. The photographer has managed to illustrate one of the causes of this disappearance, the carting away of large quantities of sand for all kinds of use. The public believed that the sand on the sea-shore was everlasting and would never run down. Despite various efforts involving the construction of groins and breakwaters it has proved impossible to retain the sand from which the resort received its name.

DUNLUCE CASTLE, CO. ANTRIM (WAG 2913)

Dunluce Castle, while not being the oldest castle in Ulster, is certainly the most impressive. The ruins cover almost an acre of ground and the cliffs on which it stands are washed on three sides by the sea. The cliffs are nearly one hundred feet above the sea and in some places the castle walls are built flush with the cliff face, making it impossible for attackers to scale it. It is likely because of this that the fortification got the name Dunluce which means strong fortress. Its position on a basaltic outcrop separated from the mainland by a twenty foot wide chasm made it practically impregnable.

DUNLUCE CASTLE, CO. ANTRIM (WAG 2863A)

The early history of Dunluce Castle has been lost in the mists of time but it would seem likely that a fortification of some sort existed from the earliest times. The name Dunluce suggests that it is a fortification of great antiquity. It had probably seen service as an Iron Age promontory fort but the first mention of Dunluce occurs about 1102 when it was attacked by Magnus Barefoot, King of Norway. The occupant of the castle at that time was Cooey O'Flynn.

DUNLUCE CASTLE (WAG 356)

Cooey O'Flynn was succeeded by his son and then by his grandson, Rory, who died in 1215. The O'Flynn lineage disappears and the Normans under Richard de Burgo rebuilt Dunluce *circa* 1305 and installed Richard de Mandeville as constable. The castle, which resembled Norman castles like Harlech and Conway in Wales, originally consisted of five circular towers which were defended by bowmen. These towers were connected by strong curtain walls with a gallery running round the top and battlements pierced at intervals for archers.

DUNLUCE CASTLE (WAG 356A)

The de Mandevilles remained in possession of Dunluce for some years and in the course of time they appear to have changed their name to MacQuillan. It is thought that the name derived from MacHughlin, meaning son of little Hugh (de Mandeville). Even at the present time in County Antrim, Hughie is pronounced Qughie, hence MacQuilin or MacQuillan. It is debatable whether the MacQuillans are descended from the Norman family of de Mandevilles or not but there is no doubt that they subsequently became more Irish than the Irish themselves. The MacQuillans continued to occupy the castle until the battle of Orra in 1559 when they were defeated by the MacDonnells who occupied Dunluce until it was abandoned about 1660.

DUNLUCE CASTLE (WAG 2169A)

The Earl of Antrim's wife (the former Duchess of Buckingham) had been accustomed to entertaining on a grand scale. On a stormy October night in 1639 she welcomed about thirty invited guests to Dunluce Castle. Stormy nights were not unusual around Dunluce so no one paid any heed. During dinner there was a resounding crash and the kitchen quarters with the cook and eight servants were precipitated into the sea below. A tinker or tinsmith who one minute was sitting quietly mending pots and pans on the sill of an alcove, found himself with nothing between him and a one hundred foot drop into the raging sea below. Lady Antrim refused to stay in Dunluce another night.

CAUSEWAY TRAM AT DUNLUCE (WAG 1875)

As might be expected, Dunluce Castle was a recognised stopping place for travellers to the Causeway. It was not a prolonged stop but one sufficiently long to allow the tram conductors to tell some of the tales of characters and events connected with the castle, such as the romance of Colla MacDonnell and Evelyn MacQuillan, the ghost of Maeve Roe, the Duchess of Buckingham and the collapse of the castle kitchen, and stories of Sorley Boy MacDonnell and Shane O'Neill.

CLOUGHORR HOUSE, PORTRUSH (WAG 126)

Cloughorr House was probably at one time the only big house on the outskirts of Portrush on the road leading from Bushmills. It later became Cloughorr Hotel and the proprietor was Mrs Rankin. The Rankins also had a dairy and what would be called today a "milk-run". A short time after the Royal Portrush Golf Club moved to Bushmills Road, the hotel was renamed the Golf Links Hotel. In more recent years several extensions have been added and the complex, now known as Kellys, includes Kelly's Golf Links Hotel, a caravan site and a leisure centre.

METROPOLE HOTEL (WAG 200)

The Metropole Corner was always regarded as one of the hazards of the North-West 200 Motorcycle Race and as a result the hotel was a very popular spot from which to see the thrills and spills of the race. The hotel became the offices of the Ulster Savings Movement at the beginning of World War II and in the early seventies the Northern Health and Social Services Board acquired it for an old people's residential home. More recently the top floor has been taken over by the community health section of the Board.

THE EAST STRAND, PORTRUSH (WAG 502)

The east strand in Portrush probably attracts more visitors than any other strand in Ireland. This is hardly surprising since the clear blue water with its billowing waves looks so inviting to swimmers and bathers. Even those who came unprepared to take a 'dip' could roll up their trouser legs or hoist their skirts and venture in for a paddle, whilst would be Steve Donahues or Gordon Richards could go for a ride on one of the donkeys.

KERR STREET FROM THE HARBOUR, PORTRUSH
(WAG 237)

Like so many of the streets in Portrush, Kerr Street faces the sea. It was named, as was Mark Street, after Lord Mark Kerr MacDonnell, the Earl of Antrim, who was the landlord of Portrush. The yacht CE 126 was built locally in Kelly's Boatyard.

NORTHERN COUNTIES HOTEL, PORTRUSH (WAG 239)

This hotel has been referred to as "the heart of Portrush." It was built in 1837 as the "Antrim Arms Hotel" and when the Northern Counties railway came to the town in 1855, the directors of the railway took over the hotel and enlarged it. Edwin Waugh writing in 1856 describes it as *"a grand hotel catering for lords, dukes, judges"*. Among its patrons was H.R.H. Prince Arthur, Duke of Connaught, who stayed there while on a visit to the Giant's Causeway in 1860. The hotel was reconstructed in 1892 to designs by John Lanyon architect, and the rear was extended in 1894 by Berkeley D. Wise, the Railway Company's engineer. Unfortunately this fine building was burned down in 1990.

SS HAZEL AT PORTRUSH (WAG 367)

The *Hazel* was known locally as the "Scotch Boat" and her daily arrival in the resort caused a great deal of excitement. A ship of 1200 tons capable of a speed of 19 knots, she was built in 1907 to operate a daily daylight crossing from Ardrossan to Portrush. When the occasion warranted, the *Hazel* called at Ballycastle where the passengers were ferried in or out by rowing boat. The return fare in 1909 was 12s 6d. The sailings came to an end with the outbreak of the First World War.

MOUNT ROYAL, PORTRUSH (WAG 373)

Mount Royal may have been built in 1900 as a terrace of very fine four-storey houses but in order to accommodate Portrush's rapidly increasing tourist population they were converted into private hotels. They all called themselves Mount Royal prefixed with the house number, e.g. 3 Mount Royal. The end house, as well as having excellent views from the front and side, had a dove-cote at the building in the rear. One wonders if pigeon-pie was on the menu.

SEABANK HOUSE AND BATH TERRACE (WAG 374)

Seabank House was built *c*1890 and situated as it was so close to the sea with an uninterrupted view of the bay, it was inevitable that it should become Seabank Hotel. In 1937 it advertised:— *"Charming position; Own grounds; Ocean front; Convenient for all sports; Excellent catering and service; Bathing from the Hotel;* *H. and C. in all rooms; Central heating; Electric lift; Ballroom; Orchestra."* It became a hall of residence for students of the New University of Ulster in 1967 and is now (1990) a high-quality private residential home.

LADIES BATHING PLACE, PORTRUSH (WAG 503)

The building here is the Arcadia which has been a cafe and dance hall and conference centre. The first building on this site was a wooden hut, and this was replaced by a substantial building erected by R. A. Chalmers, a prominent business-man in the resort, who was also chairman of Portrush Urban District Council. The balcony above the cafe was used for open-air dancing. A weighing machine and a metal embossing printer (a novelty at the time) stand outside the cafe. A Royal Navy destroyer on a courtesy visit to the resort is anchored in the Skerry Roads.

THE STRAND, PORTRUSH (WAG 2862A)

This sheltered spot was a favourite with elderly visitors. It was not too far from the shops and the boarding houses, and the Arcadia Cafe was convenient for a friendly cup of tea. The Arcadia has been photographed repeatedly to record the many additions and improvements which have taken place. Many of those who remember the Arcadia as a "ballroom of romance" regret the fact that it has now been converted into a leisure centre.

AT THE BLUE POOL, PORTRUSH (WAG 506)

The Blue Pool was one of the most popular bathing places in the resort. Its clear, cool, Atlantic water and its natural rock amphitheatre for spectators made it an ideal venue for diving displays and swimming galas which were organised every week during July and August. Interest in aquatic exhibitions began to wane in the fifties and such events are now a thing of the past.

LANDSDOWNE CRESCENT FROM THE SOUTH
(WAG 507)

These fine three and four storey houses served as excellent private hotels for Portrush's influx of summer visitors. The term "private hotel" might suggest that they were small but that was not the case. For instance the "Skerry-Bhan" which was owned by the Carson family had 60 bedrooms. "The York", "Dunard", "Tower House" and others all had one thing in common — they provided first-class accommodation and good food. Unfortunately the proprietors had no control over the weather which was not too good, judging from the wrapped up visitors on the summer-seats.

MARK STREET, PORTRUSH (WAG 508)

Another Portrush street called after Lord Mark Kerr. These three and four-storey houses were built in the second half of the last century as residences for prominent professional and business people. In the course of time, as Portrush's popularity as a seaside resort increased, many of them were converted into guest houses. Two adjoining houses were successfully converted into a very popular hotel — The West Bay View.

KERR STREET FROM ACROSS THE HARBOUR
(WAG 509)

Kerr Street is seen here with Mark Street towering above on the higher ground. The main feature of the photograph is the fishing boat under sail. In the days before the petrol or diesel engine small boats were solely propelled by wind or oar. This vessel was probably built at James Kelly's Boatyard in Portrush.

KERR STREET, PORTRUSH (WAG 509A)

This is a companion picture to that on the previous page and it looks as if they were both taken on the same morning. The trawl warps can be seen in the photograph which suggests that the vessel is still fishing although it is almost alongside the quay. Could the explanation be that the photographer had requested the fishermen to show the vessel in its working position?

PORTRUSH FROM THE HARBOUR (WAG 360)

This view from the harbour dates from before World War I and the old dock — the town's first harbour — can be seen in the foreground. The bridge carried a railway line for coal wagons from the station down to the quayside. The railway station with its large cafe, which was used for all kinds of functions, stands in the background. The Pleasure Gardens to the right of the cafe were a financial flop but that does not prevent people from remembering them with nostalgia.

CAUSEWAY/EGLINTON STREET, PORTRUSH (WAG 510)
A busy street with signs of various forms of transport — tram lines for the Causeway Tram, horse traffic including jaunting-cars and spring-carts. At the top right stands the Methodist Church with its spire. A drinking fountain with a canopy can be seen to the left of the photograph and what looks like a dove-cote is further left against the back of the large house.

CAUSEWAY STREET, PORTRUSH (WAG 511)

This loaded tram is heading down Causeway Street towards Bushmills and the Giant's Causeway. Despite the fact that poles carrying the electricity for the tramway can be seen along the footpath, the tram is being pulled by a small steam-engine. This was because the local urban council refused to allow electric power to be used within the town boundary. The street lamps are lighted with gas from the council's gasworks. The dress of the couple on the left in their Edwardian costumes suggests that the period is between 1901 and 1910.

GOLF TERRACE, PORTRUSH (WAG 512)

This fine terrace, facing the West Strand and convenient to the old golf course, was built in 1880, but the view from many of them must have been marred when the station buildings were erected in 1892. The Eglinton Hotel as well as the spire of the Church of Ireland church can be seen at the end of the street on the left hand side. The man with the handcart appears to be bringing visitors' luggage from the station.

WEST STRAND, PORTRUSH (WAG 514)

Considerable change has taken place at the West Strand since W. A. Green took this photograph. Serious coastal erosion made it necessary for the Urban Council to construct a promenade along the entire length of the strand. The Golf Hotel still stands, with its name changed to Castle Erin. It was occupied during the Second World War by the Ministry of Education which had been moved from Belfast, and at the end of hostilities became the headquarters of the Christian Endeavour Movement. The Skating Rink has long since disappeared as well as the Pleasure Gardens, and Barry's Amusements stand on the same site.

MIDLAND STATION, PORTRUSH (WAG 364)

William Dargan constructed the railway to Portrush in 1855 but these elaborate station buildings were not erected until 1982. They were designed in Stockbrokers' Tudor by the railway's engineer, Berkeley D. Wise; the builders were McLaughlin and Harvey of Belfast and the cost just over £10,000. Evidence of several forms of transport is included in the photograph — jaunting cars, hand carts for luggage, a motor-car, the Causeway tram and of course the train. The entrance to the Pleasure Grounds is seen on the right of the photograph close to the Station Cafe.

MAIN STREET, PORTRUSH (WAG 210)

One of the features of Portrush which city people seem to appreciate is the fact that they are nearly sure to meet their friends on one of the crowded streets. The picture would almost suggest that Main Street was a pedestrian precinct in the days before the term was invented. The shops in view include the Portrush House, famous for its Irish Linen, Macauley's Chemists, the City Hotel, Black's Trocadero Restaurant and with its conical tower, the Northern Bank, designed by Vincent Craig. Notice that most of the men are wearing caps.

MAIN STREET, PORTRUSH (WAG 361)

This view from the opposite end of Main Street must have been
taken in the off-season or early on a Sunday as it lacks the crowd
and bustle of the previous picture. It includes a number of
important land marks such as the Northern Counties Hotel with one
of its bow windows just evident on the extreme right. The building
with a portico at the end of the picture on the right is the White
House, Portrush's most prestigious store, opened on May 1st 1891
by Mr Henry Hamilton, who also owned the Windsor and White
House Hotels. On the left stands Caskey's drapery and fancy goods
shop with its canopy over the footpath.

THE WHITEROCKS, PORTRUSH (WAG 358)

Portrush streets were always crowded with day-trippers but the long-stay visitors were more likely to seek the pleasures of the more scenic spots such as the Whiterocks, which were the subject of many an artist's canvas. From the town to the Whiterocks was a comfortable distance of about a mile and a half and did not require any strenuous effort. The people in our picture are suitably garbed to withstand the fresh breezes blowing in from the Atlantic.

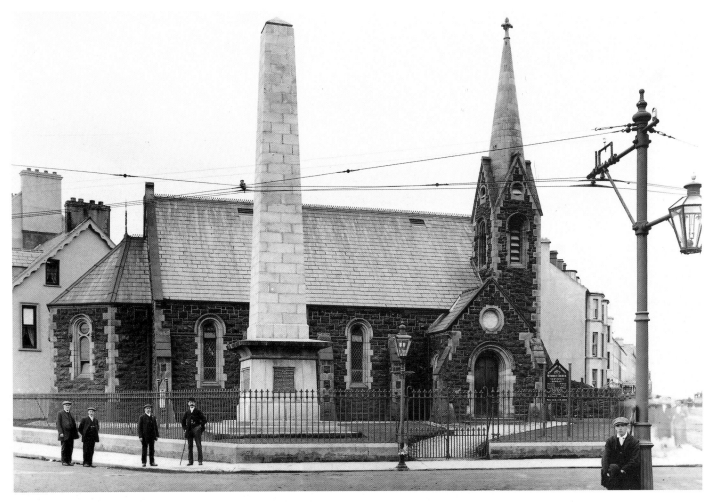

METHODIST CHURCH, PORTRUSH (WAG 369)

This fine blackstone church was erected in 1887 to replace an earlier building, which had served as a school on weekdays and a church on Sundays, from 1832. The basalt for the building came from local quarries (probably Craigahullier) and the pleasantly contrasting dressings round the windows and spire were of Ballycastle sandstone or freestone. The granite obelisk was first erected in 1859 on a mound near the old church, as a memorial to Rev. Dr Adam Clarke, the founder of Methodism in Portrush. It was re-erected in its present position in 1910 and unfortunately tends to overshadow the church.

PORTSTEWART (WAG 820)

This picture of Portstewart c1910 shows the sea-front before the famous Portstewart Promenade was built. The earliest harbour was built in 1832 by John Cromie, one of the landlords in the area. It was reconstructed by the Board of Works in 1889 at a cost of £4,000 of which £500 was subscribed by John Cromie's widow. By 1910 the harbour was proving inadequate for the booming fishing industry and a major reconstruction was undertaken which made Portstewart one of the safest harbours on the north coast.

LADIES BATHING PLACE AND BEACH, PORTSTEWART (WAG 821)

Portstewart has a fine strand just beyond the town and yet some people preferred to bathe at the west end of the front. This area later became known as the "duck-pond" and at an even later stage was converted into a proper swimming pool. More recently it became so silted up with sand and rocks that it was suitable only as a children's paddling pool. In this picture a crowd has gathered to watch a pierrot troupe in an open sided hut. At a later date the audience was able to sit on the steps at the end of the newly constructed promenade to enjoy the show.

PORTSTEWART FROM THE SEA (WAG 822)

John Cromie, the landlord of the Cromie Estate, provided the finance for Portstewart's first harbour and built and leased the village's first hotel, the Montagu Arms. He also established a bathing facility with a view to creating a seaside resort. He would not, however, allow the L.M.S. N.C.C. Railway Company to bring the railway into the town in case it would alter the quiet character of the resort. Instead he provided a tram from the town to Cromore Halt. The tram, pulled by a steam engine, can be seen in the picture passing the Montagu Arms Hotel.

MAIN STREET AND ESPLANADE, PORTSTEWART (WAG 823)

The sea-front at Portstewart is more commonly known as "The Promenade". The tall mock-Tudor building on the right was the terminus for the Portstewart tram and it was designed by Berkeley D. Wise, who had been the architect of Portrush railway station. This was conveniently built beside the Montagu Arms Hotel. Just beyond the hotel is the Bath House built by Cromie and operated by Mrs McIlreavy at the end of the century. The benefits of salt-water bathing were being loudly acclaimed, and hot and cold baths were available. The water was pumped from the sea just across the street via an underground pipe.

PORTSTEWART CASTLE (WAG 824)

Portstewart had two landlords, John Cromie and Henry O'Hara. Cromie built up the east end of the town and O'Hara the west. Probably to demonstrate his superiority O'Hara built Portstewart Castle in 1834 on the cliff-top, overlooking Cromie's town. At the time of the Famine (1846/7) a high wall was built around the castle grounds to provide work as a "famine-relief scheme". Ironically the castle came into the possession of the Montagus, who had inherited the Cromie Estate through the marriage of Miss Cromie to Lord Robert Montagu.

PORTSTEWART CASTLE (WAG 2903)

A second view of Portstewart Castle shows it being extended, probably by the Dominican order of nuns which acquired the castle in 1917 as a boarding school for girls. There have been many additions to the building over the years, as the school became one of Ulster's leading educational establishments. The castle is now only a small part of the complex. The thatched houses below the castle were known as Bone Row probably because the thatch was made secure with animal bones instead of wooden pegs. The swimming pool in the middle of the photograph has been improved with the addition of a slide and diving board.

ROCK CASTLE, PORTSTEWART (WAG 1806)

Rock Castle is thought to have been built by Henry O'Hara as a dower house for his widowed mother, and it may also have been let as a holiday villa or as a bathing lodge in the fashion of the time. It was leased to James and Frances White of Whitehall, County Antrim in the summer of 1835 and it was here that their second son, George, was born on 6th July. This son later became world-famous as Field Marshal Sir George White, V.C., who was responsible for the relief of Ladysmith on 28th February 1900.

PROMENADE, PORTSTEWART (WAG 1802)

Portstewart's popularity as a resort has resulted from its closeness to the sea. There are few resorts in which the tourist can be so close to the main shopping centre and at the same time alongside the sea. In this photograph, three of Portstewart's four churches are visible on the skyline: from the right with its towering spire the Presbyterian Church; the Clarke Memorial Methodist church and further to the left, the Catholic church with its corrugated-iron roof. The Church of Ireland church, which is not visible, stands in the Diamond to the right of the picture.

MAIN FRONT, PORTSTEWART (WAG 1803)

Portstewart's Promenade is only one of its assets; it also has a fine strand (see page 85). Most people holidaying in Portstewart are inclined to take advantage of both these assets, relaxing on the golden sand by day and parading up and down the promenade in the evening. John Cromie would have been pleased that Portstewart has retained most of its old character. Confectionery and minerals were sold in the temporary building on the left and there is a vacant space where the Town Hall was built later.

PORTSTEWART GOLF CLUB (WAG 1805)

It is recorded that in 1895 a number of residents in the Portstewart area decided to form a golf club. They subscribed a sum of £16 to build the wooden clubhouse shown in the photograph on the newly established course on the Portrush Road. Green fees were 3 shillings per week and in the second year the income from visitors' fees was £13-6s. The Portstewart Tram, which passed the door, provided a good service from the town to the golf course. Subsequently the course proved to be too small and a decision was taken in 1907 to acquire ground at the Strand Head for an additional 18-hole course. The old course continued to be so popular that a new clubhouse was erected in 1931 and the course was extended to 18 holes in 1932.

PORTSTEWART STRAND (WAG 1804)

Portstewart's position on the Atlantic Coast with miles of safe bathing, makes it one of the most attractive resorts in Ireland. It has the added advantage that the sand is firm and motor cars can drive on it without any danger of getting "bogged down". On a good summer day it is not unusual to see one thousand cars parked along the strand yet, people are not crammed together like sardines as they are at some continental resorts. Near the cottage on the right is a holy well known as Tubberpatrick or St Patrick's Well.

PORTSTEWART STRAND (WAG 3338)

Green's photographs of Portstewart Strand fail to give a true impression of its extent. Neither view whether taken near the entrance to the strand or looking back towards the town, manages to convey any sense of the length of it, which is more than two miles. The dune system at the top of the beach contains a varied flora and fauna as well as many items of archaeological interest. Portstewart Strand is now controlled by the National Trust and, no doubt, John Cromie would have been delighted that his efforts to preserve the character of Portstewart were still being furthered.

EXCELSIOR VILLAS, PORTSTEWART (WAG 1809)

These houses probably were named Excelsior because any new housing in the area had to move higher and higher up the rising ground above the resort. As these would have been described as "desirable residences" it is difficult to see any connection with the donkey and cart. Yet the boys on the cart and the one with the donkey look to be fairly "well-heeled". No doubt somebody somewhere knows who they are and why they have posed with this yoke.

ATLANTIC CIRCLE, PORTSTEWART (WAG 1810)

W.A. Green was probably fascinated by this curving block of houses with such an attractive name. These well-built houses performed a very useful function in the resort. Holiday accommodation in the hotels tended to be priced at a level well beyond the pocket of the average holiday-maker. Many of the houses in Atlantic Circle served as guest-houses providing comfortable accommodation for families at affordable prices.

THE CRESCENT, PORTSTEWART (WAG 1811)

The Catholic Church in Portstewart was shown in Lever Road with a corrugated-iron roof in an earlier photograph (Page 82). A new church was built at the Crescent in 1915 by Thornbury Brothers of Belfast to the designs of W. J. Moore, architect also of Belfast at a cost of £6,000. The first wedding in the new church was that of Mr A. J. Mullan of Coleraine and Miss Anne McKinney. Coincidentally their eldest son, Rev. Liam Mullan, is the present Parish Priest of Portstewart. This writer married their daughter, Moira. Portstewart was part of St Malachy's Parish in Coleraine until 1954 when it became a parish in its own right.

VICTORIA TERRACE, PORTSTEWART (WAG 1812)

It is hardly necessary to name this street as the Victorian architecture indicates the period of building. The conservatory with its scalloped edging to the roof is a feature of the time as well as the wooden porch further along. The pair of mock-Tudor houses at the end of the street, well-covered with Virginia creeper must have had a wealthy owner in their early days.

Other photographs from the W. A. Green Collection on the Ards not included in this selection.
Prints of these, and the photographs in the book, may be obtained from the photographic department of the Ulster Folk and
Transport Museum, Cultra, Co. Down.

WAG 151	Wishing Arch, Whiterocks	WAG 840	The Fan, Giant's Causeway	WAG 2197	White Rocks, Portrush
WAG 152	Whiterocks	WAG 841	Port Moon, Giant's Causeway	WAG 2216	Port Ballintrae
WAG 152A	Whiterocks	WAG 841A	Port Moon, Giant's Causeway	WAG 2217	Port Ballintrae
WAG 154	Giant's Causeway	WAG 843	Cave, Giant's Causeway	WAG 2218	Port Ballintrae
WAG 156	Organ, Giant's Causeway	WAG 844	The Causeway cliffs from the	WAG 2858	Carrick-a-Rede
WAG 157	Giant's Causeway		Chimney Pots	WAG 2862	The Strand, Portrush
WAG 159	Amphitheatre, Giant's Causeway	WAG 847	Port Braddon, Whitepark	WAG 2863	Dunluce Castle
WAG 161A	The Chimney Pots, Giant's	WAG 849	Port Ballintrae	WAG 2862B	The Strand, Portrush
	Causeway	WAG 850	Port Ballintrae	WAG 2882	Ballintoy Harbour
WAG 162	Chimney Pots, Giant's Causeway	WAG 1300	Dunluce Castle	WAG 2909	Strand, Whiterocks
WAG 164	Wishing Chair, Giant's Causeway	WAG 1421	Coast at Dunluce	WAG 2890	Bush Foot
WAG 185	The Esplanade, Portrush	WAG 1422	Dunluce Castle	WAG 2901	White Head from Dunseverick
WAG 186	Whitepark Bay	WAG 1423	Port Ballintrae		Harbour
WAG 187	Whitepark Bay	WAG 1425	Rope Bridge, Carrick-a-Rede	WAG 2916	Great Arch and Sea Stacks,
WAG 248	Lansdowne Crescent, Portrush	WAG 1765	Salmon Leap, Bushmills		Whitepark Bay
WAG 357	Barbican, Dunluce Castle	WAG 1801	Portstewart	WAG 2917	Sea Stacks, Ballintoy
WAG 359	Arch, Whiterocks	WAG 1807	Portstewart Castle	WAG 2918	Causeway Cliffs and Port Moon
WAG 365	Ramore Head, Portrush	WAG 1808	Portstewart Castle	WAG 2937A	Ballintoy Harbour and Stacks
WAG 366	Storm at the Giant's Causeway	WAG 1848	Dunluce Castle	WAG 2960	Youth Hostel, Whitepark Bay
WAG 368	Portrush Harbour and Scotch Boat	WAG 1860	Dunluce Castle	WAG 3287	Arcadia Cafe and bathing place,
WAG 370	Dunluce Castle	WAG 1861	Dunluce Castle		Portrush
WAG 371	Pleaskin Head, Giant's Causeway	WAG 1862	Dunluce Castle	WAG 3449	O'Hara's Castle, Portstewart
WAG 375	The Pleaskins, Giant's Causeway	WAG 1874	Dunluce Castle	WAG 2605	Rocks at Portrush
WAG 372	The Organ, Giant's Causeway	WAG 1888	Giant's Causeway 1822 by	WAG 3623	Ballintoy
WAG 422	Causeway Street, Portrush		J. W. Cambell	WAG 3673	Whitepark Bay
WAG 432	Causeway Street, Portrush	WAG 2020	Giant's Head, Portrush	WAG 3764	The Grand Causeway
WAG 433	The Arch of the Winds	WAG 2070	Whitepark Bay	WAG 3676	Carrick-a-Rede rope bridge
WAG 501	Portrush from the Golf Links	WAG 2072A	Portbraddon from Whitepark	WAG 3867	Portrush
WAG 504	On the sands at the salmon		Bay	WAG 3868	Portrush
	fisheries, Portrush	WAG 2072B	Portbraddon from Whitepark	WAG 3869	Arch, Whitepark Bay
WAG 513	Portrush		Bay	WAG 3871	Ballintoy
WAG 754	Whiterocks, Portrush	WAG 2166	Rock Vista, Portrush	WAG 3872	Bush River
WAG 814	Elephant Rock, Whiterocks,	WAG 2168	Rue Point, Dunseverick	WAG 3873	Coastline
	Portrush	WAG 2168A	Rue Point, Dunseverick	WAG 3875	The Loom, Giant's Causeway
WAG 815	Wishing Arch and Dunluce	WAG 2169	Dunluce Castle	WAG 3877	Giant's Causeway
WAG 816	Whiterocks, Portrush	WAG 2173	The Strand, Portrush	WAG 3878	Giant's Causeway
WAG 817	Great Cathedral Cave, Whiterocks	WAG 2196	Portrush	WAG 3879	Giant's Causeway
WAG 836	Rope Bridge, Carrick-a-Rede	WAG 2196A	Portrush	WAG 3880	Giant's Chair, Giant's Causeway
WAG 839	Rope Bridge, Carrick-a-Rede	WAG 2196B	West Strand, Portrush	WAG 3884	Rope Bridge, Carrick-a-Rede

Bibliography

The books listed below will provide further reading for those who wish to know more about the Causeway Coast; they are not a list of books consulted in the writing of this book. Much of the information in the book resulted from my having lived and worked in the area all my life and having listened (perhaps not always with sufficient attention) to those people who loved the north coast.

Anderson R. and McDonald, T. *Memories in Focus:* Vols 1, 2 and 3. Impact Printing, Coleraine and Ballycastle.

Bassett, G. H. *County Antrim: A guide and directory* 1886. Reprint Friar's Bush Press, Belfast.

Dallat, C. A. (Compiler) *McCahan's Local Histories.* Reprint Glens of Antrim Historical Society, Cushendall. Impact Printing, 1988.

Dallat, C. A. & Gibson, F. *Rooms of Time: memories of Ulster people.* Dept. of Health and Social Services, N.I. Greystone Press, Antrim, 1988.

Gwynn, S. *Highways and by-ways in Donegal and Antrim.* Macmillan, London, 1903.

Girvan, W. D. *Historic Buildings in North Antrim.* Ulster Architectural Heritage Society, Belfast, 1972.

Hill, Rev. G. *The MacDonnells of Antrim;* Reprint Glens of Antrim Historical Society, Cushendall 1976. Impact Printing.

Historic Monuments of Northern Ireland. Her Majesty's Stationery Office, 1983.

Mullin, J. E. *The Causeway Coast.* Century Services Limited, Belfast, 1974.

O'Laverty, Rev. J. *History of the Diocese of Down and Connor.* Vol. 4, Duffy & Sons, Dublin, 1887.

Richardson, Rev. A. *A Guide to Portrush, Giant's Causeway, Ballycastle and Neighbourhood.* c1905.

Special thanks are due to the Trustees of the Ulster Folk and Transport Museum for permission to reproduce the Green photographs. The high quality of the prints provided by Mr Ken Anderson and the staff of the photographic department must also be acknowledged.